UNLIMITED LIMITS
Management by One Liner
"Information shouts, Knowledge listens"

LALIT PANWAR

NewDelhi • London

BLUEROSE PUBLISHERS
India | U.K.

Copyright © Lalit Panwar 2024

All rights reserved by author. No part of this publication may be reproduced, stored in a retrieval system or transmitted in any form or by any means, electronic, mechanical, photocopying, recording or otherwise, without the prior permission of the author. Although every precaution has been taken to verify the accuracy of the information contained herein, the publisher assumes no responsibility for any errors or omissions. No liability is assumed for damages that may result from the use of information contained within.

BlueRose Publishers takes no responsibility for any damages, losses, or liabilities that may arise from the use or misuse of the information, products, or services provided in this publication.

For permissions requests or inquiries regarding this publication, please contact:

BLUEROSE PUBLISHERS
www.BlueRoseONE.com
info@bluerosepublishers.com
+91 8882 898 898
+4407342408967

ISBN: 978-93-6783-765-8

Cover Design: Shubham
Typesetting: Sagar

First Edition: November 2024

About Author

Author is a Business Management Professional, Entrepreneur and Educationist, having corporate and personal experience of over 25 years.

He has always been a student of practical experiences of management and tried successfully to get the theory out of them. The author feels that management starts from the point when one begins to have understanding of the basics of life and it is never ending. It is inside out reflection of facing the exposure and having meaningful experience.

He has been a follower of 'Challenge the Status Quo' principle and is in search of basics of Management.

"The me I see the me I will be"
Dr. Robert Shuller

This book is dedicated to all the Future Managers, Entrepreneurs and those who are not either and want to learn Management.

Foreword

"The origin of human beings is the only miracle in this world, rest are creations either by nature or humans."

Every word has a meaning.

Every line carries a message.

Every story tells an event of a lifetime.

You will find learning and wisdom at every step of your life. To grab it, you need to be religiously focused and observant. Even at the last stage of life, one learns about worldly separation, while at the same time learns how to live more. Therefore, learning is endless.

Everything written in this book is already known to you, and my only submission is, give some time to yourself to recollect it.

If you go slow, you will reach sooner than others.

"Wish you a happy learning"

Dr. Umakant Panwar (I.A.S.)

Acknowledgements

All the credit goes to the readers of this book, as without readers there is no meaning of writing a book.

While writing this book, three people I disturbed the most, Roma Panwar, Arundhati Panwar, and Aaryan Panwar.

Special thanks to Dr. Umakant Panwar (IAS), Er. Yogesh Panwar, Dr. Vinay Panwar, Deep Chandra and Tushar Dauthal and Vijender Badgujar.

Abhishek Panwar (Canada) and Yamini Panwar (Germany) have been good advisors for this project.

Sultan and Shon have always been with me during the journey.

A Note on the book

Management is all about People, Process and Positioning. Deep understanding of these three can lead anyone to success. I also realised this late and consequentially got late into everything in my life.

This book is just tip of the iceberg of learning management or in other words this is the starting point of understanding management.

There is no right time to learn anything but starting early can be always be a better option.

This book addresses the very basics of People, Process and Positioning. All other Ps will be easy to understand after having understanding of these 3 Ps. In fact understanding of A to Z of Management will go through these 3 Ps.

Contents

PART – I PEOPLE 1

Chapter – 1
Self 2

Chapter – 2
Observation 6

Chapter – 3
Value 10

Chapter – 4
Focus 14

Chapter – 5
Foresight and Insight 18

Chapter – 6
Approach and Attitude 22

Chapter – 7
Style & Culture 26

Part – II PROCESS 31

Chapter – 8
Fundamentals 32

Chapter – 9
Understand Category 36

Chapter – 10
System Centric Approach 40

Chapter – 11
Anticipating the Unanticipated 44

Chapter – 12
No Trail & Error 48

Chapter – 13
  Avoid Knee Jerks 52

Chapter – 14
  Technology for Efficiency Not for People Replacement 56

PART – III POSITIONING 61

Chapter – 15
  Be the First.. 62

Chapter – 16
  Differentiation with Distinction 66

Chapter – 17
  Me Too Approach Kills.. 70

Chapter – 18
  Highlight Yourself – Clear & Loud 74

Chapter – 19
  Take Care of Your Weaknesses 78

Chapter – 20
  Deliver Commitment and Strengthen Your Position 82

Chapter – 21
  Guard Your Reputation 86

PART – I
PEOPLE

"Success of an organization is directly proportional to the growth of its people"

Lalit Panwar

Chapter I

Self

"He who feels knows everything, understands nothing"

Anonymous

'Knowing your Self'
is the best among all the other achievements;
You can do wonders.

First impression tells about personality,
second tells character;
Every impression is important.

Your degree or profession is not your identity,
don't mislead yourself and others,

The way I see in you, the way I believe in you;
Show me your qualities from day one.

Self-awareness, Self-analysis, Self-motivation and more, life starts and ends with self;
First 'Manage your Self'.

Mindset is developed by self;
Skillset is learned from others.

*Difference between Rational and Irrational is 'I (Ego)',
remove 'I' and become rational.*

*You are the world not just part of it,
ask your loved ones.*

*I am healthy means
mentally, physically, emotionally and financially;
that too in the same order.*

*The moment you realize 'you can do it',
'You will do it'.*

*Those who invest in people,
become leaders in no time,
and get compounding returns.*

You own and can control, only 'Yourself'.

*I can eat on your behalf but you won't be healthy,
do it yourself;
'Procrastination Kills'.*

*Having no strategy
is the best strategy in uncertain times,
it works.*

*It is not important in how much time
but from where you started
and in what conditions you achieved the success.*

*I was stupid and wrong, realised very late;
Still, I have good enough time
for self-improvement and becoming successful.*

Chapter – 2
Observation

"Observe, give meaning to what you see"
Lalit Panwar

I see falling apple, Newton sees Gravity;
This is what observation is.

The difference between 'Seeing and Observing'
is same as eating and digesting.

Emotions are 'Reflections of Feelings',
and tell the whole story.

Capability without Reliability
is like pond without water.

Opportunity comes in different 'Forms and Directions'
than we expect, 'Be Observant'.

Anything like 'Something for Nothing',
does not exist.

*People problems become business problems,
If remain unattended, beware.*

*Someone buying from you doesn't mean,
you are always good,
there may be some compulsions, Observe.*

*You know yourself better than anybody else,
You heard it right, go check yourself.*

*You are the outcome of your decisions,
observe the decisions you are taking now.*

*Leaders are ordinary people,
with extraordinary observational ability.*

*Management means visualizing the right things
and executing them physically without gaps.*

*Creative visualization is the source of greatest creations,
first in the mind and then physically.*

*Successful people are the same as you are,
also started in the same manner.*

*Stillness is the only vibration in this world,
rest all are disturbances.*

*Loneliness, isolation and peace are three different things, but peace
brings satisfaction.*

Chapter – 3
Value

"Value if cant be lived is just a statement"
Lalit Panwar

Everyone is successful;
Only definition and degree is different.

Salary never motivates a person,
Appreciation surely does.

It is OK, until it is a matter of life or death;
Give weightage to the thing or person as the worth is.

Time is the only asset in this world.

You can train a leader provided he is one from within;
Leadership is imbibed and lived but can't be exhibited.

Adding 'Extra to Ordinary'
converts it into 'Extraordinary'.

No gain is any gain if coupled with a regret.

Heart remains pure until "I" (Ego) makes it impure.

*You can never get a better half,
until your own half gets better.*

*World will remember me not for what I got,
but I gave.*

*Reward or regret we will get in the end,
better choose it now.*

*Choosing values over valuables,
is the first step towards success.*

Organizational values,
are mirror image of a leader's belief system;
(TATA – Trust).

Do not hire a person,
whose values do not match with yours.

High 'Return on Time (ROT)' for employee means
high 'Productivity and Loyalty'.

Hire people not papers,
people exhibit values papers don't.

A value has got value till the time it is valued,
Otherwise, it is everything but value.

Work is labour when done out of compulsion,
Work is service when done for contribution.

Chapter – 4

Focus

"Have no regret, it kills before you die"
                                    Lalit Panwar

*You are your Autobiography,
become as you want it to be.*

When efforts become effortless, something big happens.

Success demands focus.

*If you can read between the lines,
don't waste time
in finding the grammatical mistakes of others.*

*You lose identity,
if try to become everything to everyone.*

*Mahatma Gandhi, Nelson Mandela, Mother Teresa,
Google and Microsoft, have one thing in common, 'Focus'.*

*Money, riches and wealth are three different things,
decide what you want.*

Growth is tangible, prerequisites are intangible.

*Universal reality is 'Time is Eternal'
And worldly is 'Time is available to All'
but the ground reality is 'We do not have Time'.*

*I expected returns more than I worked,
my focus was on returns, I was at fault!*

*Common goal is enough for team building,
Trust and Clarity bring connectedness.*

*Balloon goes up in the sky not because of colour,
but due to the substance (air) inside.*

Company was looking for a 'True Leader',
I was looking only a 'Leadership Role',
I realised that late.

Wherever you go, whatever you do,
your footprints talk everything about you.

A minute deviation of an aeroplane from its flight route,
will land it miles away from its destination.

From ignorance to awareness lies learning in between;
'Awareness is a bliss' while 'Ignorance a curse'.

Chapter – 5

Foresight and Insight

"Future is now, shape it as you want it to be"
                              Lalit Panwar

'Ask' and your learning starts,
there and then.

Becoming rich is neither a Science nor an Art,
but an ability of foresightedness.

Every great company started as a start-up,
and when someone says most of the start-ups fail,
Either he is a failure or doesn't know the business.

Your business is the outcome of the decisions taken,
if not satisfied,
change your decisions and status will change.

You know yourself better than anyone else in this world;
Still looking for others to tell about you.

'Think Ahead and Stay Ahead'
is the new success mantra.

*Only result can tell the appropriate time taken in any decision,
take decision and know it yourself.*

Decision is better than the regret of not taking it.

*'What' and 'Why' anything will happen,
can be understood by a leader with futuristic mind set.*

*Present is all I have,
past never was and future never will be.*

*What landed me in trouble was not lack of knowledge,
but lack of foresightedness.*

*Highlight your strengths,
but not weaknesses of your competitor,
it has mirror effect.*

The journey from good to great requires foresightedness.

*Instead of thinking what others think,
if we feel what others feel,
problems will disappear even before they appear.*

*Journey of becoming an entrepreneur,
sees double the lows than ups, but finally strikes gold.*

Chapter – 6
Approach and Attitude

"People are hired for skills and fired for Attitude"
Shiv Khera

Winners do the same,
which others also want but don't do.

Superiority over others,
starts with inferiority complex.

Mindset is vehicle and skillset the driver,
wish you a happy journey!

Earning money is the first step,
saving and investing will make you wealthy.

Procrastination ensures
that you pay the price but don't get value.

Negative mind does enough self-damage,
nothing else is required.

Desired output without required inputs is impossible.

*Everybody is clever,
but how many are wise is a question mark.*

*Behind any accident, there is irresponsible behaviour,
which could have been avoided in 99% of the cases.*

*Difference between getting prepared or repaired,
is as the gain or loss.*

*It is never too late to say 'sorry I misunderstood you',
and give other person a chance to say the same.*

*I was an Idiot,
proved many times but the arrogance led me down.*

Who doesn't know what I know,
Still I think I know better, attitude problem.

Separate 'I' from Immature and it becomes I'm mature.

At any point of life-cycle or business-cycle,
there is always some scope to grow.

Sabotage?
check that the greed was from both the sides,
no point of blaming, move on!

Three things can do anything and everything in this world,
those are people, people and people.

Chapter – 7

Style & Culture

"Expression creates Impression"
               Lalit Panwar

Are you sure,
you get second chance to make first impression?

Empathy not sympathy, builds organizational culture.

When an employee works with ownership mindset
and owner with employee mindset, miracle happens.

Quitability is the worst ability,
it makes you quit when you are about to succeed.

'Simplicity is the Ultimate Style',
gets differentiated among the copycats.

First the leader creates the culture of the organisation,
then culture creates the style of the team.

*Instead of doing things the way they are done,
I do it my way and face failures.*

Style brings differentiation, culture brings prosperity.

*'It is not my Job' culture spoils the whole organization,
much before you anticipate it.*

*ABC (Attendance Based Compensation),
is the first mistake an organization does;
it leads to bigger ones.*

*Myth is that start-ups need innovation,
the fact is that old businesses need it more.*

*Credit or discredit goes to the leader for the culture,
as he walks the talk or lack of it, team just follows.*

Sportspersons practice five years for five minutes of performance, what are you up to?

HR in an organization is like the nervous system, minor blockage can lead to major breakdown.

Avoid mixing the negative habit with the positive one, it neutralises the outcome.

Part – II
PROCESS

"Input determines output"
— *Lalit Panwar*

Chapter – 8
Fundamentals

"Fundamentals are the launching pads"
Lalit Panwar

*Learning is the habit,
to have all the habits which bring success.*

*People become assets or liabilities,
the way they are shaped by the organisation they join.*

*Health and Habits are prerequisites for success,
I mean 'good'.*

*Performance of an individual,
can always be taken to the next level;
human potential is unlimited.*

Financial gains are by-products of efforts and intentions.

An organisation is as stable as its fundamentals are.

Organisation expects responsibility,
employee expects authority;
But 'responsibility and authority' go hand in hand.

First 'Know Your Employee'
then 'Know Your Customer'.

Senior expects subordinates
to share everything in advance
but keep his plan as secret, case of faulty leadership.

Productivity increases not because of working hours,
but because of working environment.

Employee loyalty comes with organisational loyalty,
which is rare.

I, me, myself then you can't be a team player
but team is must to win the game, decide.

*If you can't manage yourself,
what else you would on this earth? forget organisation.*

*The highway is never one way,
if yes, then it is only my way.*

*Machine gives output,
Manager brings outcome,
Leader ensures output and outcome.*

Leadership is not to command but to follow.

Chapter – 9
Understand Category

"No two businesses or persons can be 100% same"
Lalit Panwar

Winning and remaining at top means, 're-branding'.

*Organisation doesn't mean 'who will get what out of it',
instead, who will add value at what cost.*

*Always operate in zero or one
and get returns in the same manner.*

*First 'Know Yourself',
then 'Know Your Competitor'.*

*Create a niche in a category and enjoy,
until it reaches to the potential for another niche.*

*It is better to be king of a smaller territory,
than becoming just another captain in a larger army.*

Customers' perception establishes a brand, not sale.

*Sentiments in marketplace decide,
which rung on the ladder you will be.*

*You can't have two positions of the same brand
in consumers' mind.*

*Like law of the land,
every market has its own mechanism to operate, understand.*

*Fear of competition,
your competitor is carrying more than you,
concentrate on your strengths.*

*Adjust, align and advertise,
no other way to remain relevant.*

Perform or perish, no choice left.

*In a category,
if you are not the best but most preferred one,
then your job is done.*

*Everything has a life span,
check which stage at is your brand.*

Chapter – 10

System Centric Approach

"Inventory means profit or loss lying in packed state, System and Processes are the key"

Lalit Panwar

*You don't need to reinvent the wheel,
understand how it rotates and keep moving it.*

*We are conditioned to do the job the way we have been doing, instead,
the way it should be done in present scenario.*

*Destination is static,
journey is dynamic,
enjoy both.*

*A leader takes the organization to a level,
after that, in the absence of system,
even he can't move it ahead.*

*A system has many processes
and each process has a unique system,
understand and align yourself.*

*Datamatics can become the core of organizational excellence, reduce,
TAT (Turn Around Time).*

*Without system,
it is like playing the game of 'Ladder and Snake'.*

*Organizational sustainability with profitability is not possible, if the,
organization is person centric.*

*Moving ahead is foremost,
but what about direction and control?*

*It is easy to influence a person but not the system,
avoid personal dependency.*

Every system must have alarms and signals.

*Beaten path can be a tested one,
but can't be the best, explore.*

Assembly line applies even in intellectual jobs as well.

If your system is not trustworthy, how can you be?

*Speed will be the only differentiation,
   if other things are same.*

Chapter – 11

Anticipating the Unanticipated

"Unexpected always happens"

Anonymous

*Successful business leader expects the unexpected,
for rest of the things, he has managers.*

*Newton's 3rd law always works in business and relation,
you will get an equal and opposite reaction.*

*As the blood is to body,
cash is to business,
periodical check-up and certain level are must.*

*We can't manage time,
can manage only ourselves with time.*

*Take decisions on gut feelings,
if more than 90% of the decisions already taken are proven good.*

*Calculation is simple,
you get what you have paid for.*

Preparation brings certainty in uncertain times.

*Target competition at most unexpected point,
not the weakest one.*

*Values and qualities are for difficult times,
rest of the times money works.*

*It is rightly said that you can't expect different result,
by doing the same, do I need to repeat.*

*It is not good or bad, it is simply unexpected,
make your choices carefully.*

*Mode and Medium may change,
but God and Evil live in details.*

Understand the unsaid,
whatever said understood by all.

Every outcome is not just cause or effect,
some are ripple effects.

Me first is good,
but be ready for the criticism as well.

Chapter – 12
No Trail & Error

"Expectation kills"

Lalit Panwar

Every old thing is not bad,
some carbon pieces have become diamonds.

Don't expect machines to behave like humans,
and humans like machines,
compassion is in humans.

Planning + Preparation + Performance = Perfection
What else perfection is?

Management is an Art when you manage yourself,
Science when manage others.

Mistakes are welcomed, repetitions are not.

Where there are trials there are errors,
but learning should be documented.

Managing the same things repeatedly,
and doing the same mistakes means foolishness.

We learn from mistakes is philosophical,
reality is there is always some loss tangible or intangible.

'80/20 principle' tells,
which 20% of the things affect 80% of the productivity.

Compounding effect applies to gains as well as losses.

Every successful person will tell,
that he has taken more wrong decisions than right ones,
but all were worth taking.

Admitting mistake means,
you are at second step to become successful,
first was the realisation.

'Rule of No Rules' is OK,
if others are not dependent on you, for anything.

'Mind is the Limit', not sky.

My teacher says, 'practice does not make things perfect',
it makes things permanent whatever you practice,
only right practice does.

Chapter – 13

Avoid Knee Jerks

*"Barriers are for safety,
ignore and you will have the same opinion soon"*
Lalit Panwar

*Decisions made with 'AND' or 'OR',
decide inclusiveness or exclusiveness.*

*Business doesn't have emotions but people have,
whom are you dealing with?*

*A permanent solution to a temporary problem,
is excess usage of resources.*

*Leaders don't have any opinion,
before the final opinion.*

*It is ok to be rationally irrational at times,
for larger gains.*

*If I am OK, you are OK,
then where is the problem?*

Multiple layers of communication,
convert a 'Message' in to a 'Statement'.

Less baggage comfortable journey is a good thing.

The problems of 'I have made a rule',
can only be resolved by 'let us make a rule'.

Even the God of Cricket (Sachin Tendulkar)
did not play all the balls, some he left.

Conventional wisdom is still priceless,
lack of understanding is the problem.

Talking to machines using senses,
and to people through machines, is absurd.

*I have heard,
that no plan, no map and no fortune.*

*Train your people,
to bring solutions along with the problems.*

Challenge the status quo.

Chapter – 14

Technology for Efficiency Not for People Replacement

"Technology should highlight not hijack you"
                                        Shiv Khera

Man creates machine,
then machine asks man, 'is he a machine'?

At times facts may mislead,
it is your duty to verify the truth.

Early adoption of 'Right Technology' keeps you ahead.

Like Product and Business Life Cycle,
there is 'Technology Life Cycle', upgrade with time.

Don't get misled, data is not important,
only authentic data is.

Have 24x7 IPS (Information Processing System) for Managers,
real time decision making is possible.

*Technology replaces 'Silo Type' working
with 'Collective Wisdom'.*

*Big Data and same technology are being used
by the competitor that you are using, be careful.*

*80% of the daily jobs can be automated,
with 20% of the resources.*

*Efficiency can be multiple times, in no time,
with right technology.*

*This is false narrative,
that technology reduces the manpower.*

*In any organization,
80% of the decisions are taken on the basis of technology and rest 20%
with the help of it.*

*The man and machine are complimentary,
integration is the key.*

No technology in the world can be 100% fault free.

*Invest in people and pay for technology,
not vice versa.*

PART – III
POSITIONING

"My habit of talking much and communicating nothing is a problem"

Lalit Panwar

Chapter – 15

Be the First

"Leaders are Readers, and wealth is created from Deeper Knowledge and Better Thinking"
                                                        Andrew Carnegie

*When selling is there, then team is effective,
if buying is taking place then concept.*

*Yes, it is difficult to recall the second person
landed on Moon or climbed the Mount Everest.*

*Find the way to be the first in the category,
or develop a category.*

*Chances of the 'first becoming the best',
are always higher.*

*Let me show my loyalty first,
in thin and thick of the organisation.*

Dream and Desire then Dedicate yourself to your Decision.

Ideas are like time and tide,
once gone it is gone for ever.

Experiments becomes inventions if are ahead of time.

First communicate solution,
then create perception,
selling is last.

Don't categorise everything good or bad,
average always have scope of becoming better.

If you are the only one in the category,
create competition,
you will be valued more.

High price doesn't mean the best.

Projection is only the starting point;
end is satisfied stakeholders.

Take time if have any doubts,
you will find yourself correct either way.

Customers have preferences;
Be first to contact and convinces them, it matters.

Chapter – 16
Differentiation with Distinction

"Get a place in customer's mind, simply yours"
Lalit Panwar

'Information' shouts, 'knowledge' listens.

*World's Best Brands are not because of the complexity of offerings,
but the simplicity of the message they carry.*

*My habit of talking much and communicating little,
is a problem.*

*Winning in business is,
managing people, process and positioning.*

*Your conduct is your signature,
do it carefully.*

*Your commitment is your business card,
it matters.*

The best among equals means,
'Differentiation with Distinction'.

Odds become even,
when there is no differentiation.

I laughed on my stupidities,
what else can be done?

People have one thing in common,
we all are different.

Winners are not different,
'Habit of Doing' makes the difference.

All the great companies,
started as trustworthy companies.

*The more you know,
more you feel you don't know more.*

*Express, execute and express
that is how anything is evolved.*

*Best team is,
whose members know the blind spots of each other.*

*Winners have no excitement of success,
they are habitual of it.*

Chapter – 17
Me Too Approach Kills

*"You can be rich but not wealthy,
without understanding calculations"*

Lalit Panwar

Why do you want what others want,
give them a chance to copy you.

To generate my passive income,
I spent my many active years.

You are not a photocopy of anyone in this world.

There are differences even when the DNA is same;
Be original.

Apply me too approach,
the second one will appreciate the value of the first one.

Size of the pie is big enough,
you will find your own share.

Me too can never be anything but the best,
it's simple.

Find a better work place than yours,
talk to people over there;
Soon you will have different opinion.

My Boss is good 'but'...,
that means he is not.

I am looking for a job change means,
either your learning has stopped
or others are up to date.

Work more than you get,
soon you will get more than you work.

Countries, Companies and Consumers want the same,
the others are having, no idea why?

*Stick to that 'Single Word',
the others have in their minds about 'You'.*

Difference for the sake of difference will not sustain.

*Customers and not the celebrities,
are the real brand ambassadors.*

*All the position holders are not leaders,
but all the leaders have positions.*

Chapter – 18

Highlight Yourself – Clear & Loud

"If you will not talk about yourself, who else will
                                                Lalit Panwar

Branding is same as conveying the moral of the story.

*Success is the sum total of,
the decisions taken during the journey.*

*People may not see your prayers,
but your faith is visible to all.*

*It is a myth,
that positioning of a brand starts from market,
fact is, it starts from the shop floor.*

*Brand is what you communicate and others listen,
be clear & loud.*

*I know how startup works;
Because, I have failed thrice.*

*I am afraid of having no fear,
as fear of losing my gains always kept me ahead.*

Check, are you just a brand or brand with a difference?

*'Let us do it',
is the best way to exhibit your leadership skills.*

*You can never be the best,
without getting better what you are good at.*

*Your actual worth is much more than your net worth;
Please understand.*

*Balance Sheet is the outcome of
what you shout and people hear in the market place.*

As every number is important for a digit,
same are your words to make a brand.

You heard it right but misunderstood,
then I am at fault.

People know about you nothing more than what you conveyed.

Chapter – 19

Take Care of Your Weaknesses

"You have got the capability, check your capacity"
                                                    Lalit Panwar

Your weaknesses are your biases towards your desires.

*Behave like the one you want to become,
even when you are not that,
soon you will become the one.*

*As the chain depends on weakest link;
You team is as strong as your weakest member is.*

*The business advice we give to others,
do not apply to ourselves,
because they are not good and somewhere we know this.*

*There is no replacement of preparation and practice,
take care of your weaknesses.*

*Single matchstick can destroy the whole forest,
get the negative person out of your team, NOW.*

*Becoming admirable is not easy,
it does not come with money, post or power.*

*Say, 'I am as great to me as you are to you',
soon you will have more strengths than weaknesses.*

*The team is the strongest point of its leader,
but the leader is the weakest point of the team.*

*A leader in the category without competition,
will be exposed soon for his weaknesses, be ready.*

Defects and malfunctioning are two different things.

The one overcome his weaknesses faster than others, leads.

Customer is the only source of feedback; rest are based on it.

Yes, it is true that God and Evil live in details.

In modern world, pebbles in the thirsty crow story are the efforts being done to get out of weaknesses.

Chapter – 20

Deliver Commitment and Strengthen Your Position

"Your Commitment is your Business Card"
Lalit Panwar

Happy stakeholders,
are a guarantee of sustainability with profitability.

You are not in deep water,
you are in deep and there is water as above;
Deliver what you are supposed to do.

Even if your net worth is growing,
but your stakeholders are not happy,
soon you will be out of business.

People don't buy products;
they buy solutions or convenience.

Sale will not happen,
as you are talking about features
and customer is thinking of his pain points.

Salary never motivates a person,
appreciation and commitment surely do.

*Have futuristic approach and keep looking for good people,
you will be requiring them soon.*

*'Care' is what customer likes the most,
even more than your product.*

*No condition is good or bad, it is just that,
responsibility should be owned.*

Relationship means fulfillment of commitment.

*An average employee with reliability,
is better than the skilled with non-reliability.*

*Loyal customer postpones its buying
in case of non-availability of product,
if company has strong bonding with him.*

No client should be taken for granted.

*Customer like time and tide wait for no one,
'Innovation' is the glue.*

*People buy values not just products,
everyone involved in the delivery chain should know this.*

Chapter – 21
Guard Your Reputation

"Reputation once gone, gone forever"
                                    Lalit Panwar

You can get a reputed place but not the reputation.

*Guard your reputation like your life,
once lost can't be regained.*

Your face value is your brand value.

*If someone accepts and says, 'I don't know this',
he is trustworthy.*

*If a brand is full of commitment,
it becomes a life partner.*

*Your criticism of something talks more about you,
than the thing you criticize.*

Success understands smell of hard work only.

*While thinking of someone or something,
the single word that comes to mind is Brand Positioning.*

*If you are honest, you should look honest,
and the others should feel the same.*

Getting acceptance for your point of view is also selling.

*Organization's image is employee's foremost responsibility,
job description comes later.*

*No stick in this world can separate the water,
other than the members no one can spoil the team.*

*Saying 'It is OK',
burns all the differences.*

*If you hire an incapable person,
then who is incompetent?*

*No gain in this world,
is greater than the loss of reputation.*

www.ingramcontent.com/pod-product-compliance
Lightning Source LLC
LaVergne TN
LVHW061619070526
838199LV00078B/7348